TRUE BANK HEISTS

VOLUME ONE

THE TRUE STORIES OF
THE HATTON GARDEN &
HARRY WINSTON HEISTS

I0099944

RIC ORO

ISBN: 978-1-969899-13-3

January 2026

Contents

The following are based on a true stories; however creative liberties were taken. Portions of events are both real and fabricated for entertainment purposes to emphasize drama and suspense. Enjoy.

The Hatton Garden Heist: The Grandfather's Plan

The Long Game

The fluorescent hum of a public library in north London provided the only soundtrack to Daniel Jones's obsession. It was August 2012, and while the rest of the city was swept up in the fever of the Olympic Games, Danny's eyes were fixed on a different prize. He sat hunched over a flickering monitor, his reflection ghostly against the black text of industrial tool catalogs. To anyone passing by, he was just another pensioner checking his email; in reality, he was the architect of the most ambitious heist in English history.

Danny didn't believe in luck. He believed in physics, patience, and the cold reality of reinforced concrete. This was the beginning of a three-year masterclass in criminal preparation, and every member of his "Grandfather" gang had a specific role to play in this long, quiet game.

The Hatton Garden safe deposit vault was a fortress, a subterranean box of steel and stone that held the secrets and fortunes of the city's diamond district. Most thieves would look at the thick walls and the iron-tight security and see an impossibility. Danny looked at it and saw a math problem that would take three years to solve.

This level of patience was unheard of in the criminal underworld. While younger crews were out pulling "smash-and-grabs" for quick cash, Danny and his associates—men who had spent decades in the shadows—were playing the long game. They understood that a job of this magnitude required a foundation built on meticulous research.

As the primary researcher, Danny's first task was the most critical: finding a way through the vault's physical defenses. He spent months scouring the internet for a weapon capable of screaming through two feet of solid, reinforced concrete. He wasn't looking for a standard hardware store drill; he needed something industrial, something that could bite into the wall without shattering its own teeth.

Night after night, he logged on, his browser tabs filled with technical specifications for diamond-tipped core drills. He compared torque, RPMs, and cooling systems. He had to find a machine that was powerful enough to do the work but portable enough to be carried down a lift shaft in the dead of night.

His deep dives into the technical specifications of diamond-tipped core drills eventually led him to the **Hilti DD350**. To master it, he spent countless hours watching instructional videos on **YouTube**, memorizing the rhythm of the machine until he could practically hear the diamond bit grinding against the concrete in his sleep. He also acted as the group's amateur economist, tracking the fluctuating market

10

prices of gold and diamonds to ensure their three-year wait would be worth every second of risk.

He wasn't just guessing what was behind those vault doors; he was calculating the weight of the potential haul. He wanted to know exactly how much every kilogram of gold would be worth on the black market and how many carats it would take to ensure they never had to work again. By the time 2013 rolled around, Danny knew the value of the vault's contents better than the people who owned the boxes.

While Danny handled the technical hardware, the operation needed a seasoned leader to hold the crew together. That was **Brian Reader**, the 76-year-old veteran often called the "Mastermind". Reader was the one who provided the initial spark for the job, drawing on decades of experience in the criminal underworld. During the planning phase, he was the strategic lead, deciding which nights were best for scouting and ensuring that the gang remained "invisible" to the authorities. He was the anchor, the man who knew that in a job this big, one impulsive move could ruin years of work.

Every heist needs a way in and a way out. **John Collins**, age 74, was the man responsible for the "wheels" and the lookouts. During the three years of preparation, Collins was the primary scout. He was the one who drove the **white Mercedes** around Hatton Garden, posing as a casual visitor or a driver while he mapped out the security guard rotations and the best escape routes. His role was to understand the flow of the street—where the cameras were blind and how long it would take for a patrol car to respond to an alarm.

Then there was **Terry Perkins**, a man whose criminal history was as long as his temper was short. Perkins brought the "heavy" thieving experience to the table. While Danny researched the drills, Perkins focused on the vault's interior layout. He was the one who studied how to crack the individual safe deposit boxes once they were inside. He worked closely with

Danny to plan the physical exertion required for the job, calculating how many boxes they could smash in a single night and how to transport the heavy loot back out through the lift shaft.

Finally, there was the mystery man known only as **"Basil"**. While the others were well-known to each other, Basil was the specialist who provided the literal keys to the kingdom. His role during the preparation phase was the most secretive: he was responsible for obtaining the security codes and physical keys needed to enter the building at 88–90 Hatton Garden without having to blow the front doors off. He was the insider, the man who turned a "break-in" into an "entry".

As the planning phase entered its second year, the research moved from the digital world to the physical one. Danny and the gang began to haunt the streets of Hatton Garden. They didn't arrive in fast cars; they arrived in the morning mist, blending in with the hundreds of other tradesmen who serviced the district.

They watched the building at 88–90 Hatton Garden with the intensity of predators. They noted the exact time the security guards changed shifts. They studied the delivery entrances and the way the trash was collected. To the casual observer, they were just a group of older men—grandfathers, perhaps—sharing a quiet conversation on a street corner. But beneath the flat caps and heavy coats, they were mapping the layout of a fortress.

Every piece of information was fed back into the plan. If a guard stayed five minutes late, the timeline was adjusted. If a new camera was installed, the entry point was reconsidered.

By 2015, the three-year clock was nearing its end. The gang had spent 1,000 days preparing for a single weekend of work. They had met in quiet, nondescript pubs like The Castle, whispering over pints of ale as they synchronized their roles.

By the Easter weekend of 2015, it was a perfectly tuned machine, with every "grandfather" knowing exactly where to stand when the lights finally went out. The concrete was waiting. The gold was waiting. And the world was about to find out exactly what three years of meticulous, specialized planning could achieve.

Elderly Infiltrators

The rain over London was a cold, thin mist that blurred the neon signs of the diamond district as Thursday, April 2nd, faded into night. For most, the Easter Bank Holiday meant a quiet escape from the city; for the men huddled in the back of a nondescript white van, it was the start of a three-year-old dream becoming a high-stakes reality.

The figure slipped out of the shadows near the side entrance of 88–90 Hatton Garden. To any late-night passerby, he looked like an eccentric traveler or perhaps a theater worker, his head topped with a messy red wig and a low-slung cap. But the man known only as **"Basil"** didn't move like a tourist. He moved with the predatory grace of a ghost who owned the keys to the kingdom.

Stopping at the heavy side door, Basil didn't pull out a crowbar or a lockpick. Instead, he produced a set of keys—the result of years of meticulous, invisible preparation. The lock clicked with a sound that seemed like a gunshot in the silent street. He slipped inside, his heart thundering against his ribs, and signaled the others.

The side door creaked open just wide enough for the rest of the "Grandfathers" to slip through like shadows following a master. Danny Jones, Terry Perkins, and the others were loaded with heavy bags, their faces set in grim masks of concentration. They weren't just stepping into a building; they were stepping out of the world of the living and into a three-day clock that was already ticking.

Once inside, the silence of the building was oppressive. They knew the walls were filled with silent sentinels—sensors and alarms designed to scream at the first sign of trouble.

"Cut the lines," Danny whispered.

Working with the precision of surgeons, they located the nerve center of the building's security. With a sharp snap of industrial snips, they **severed the telephone lines**. In that instant, the building was effectively blinded and gagged. The external alert capabilities were dead. If an alarm triggered now, it would be a scream in a vacuum—no signal would reach the outside world, no police dispatch would receive the call, and no sirens would come racing through the London mist.

The most dangerous part of the entry lay ahead. The ground floor was a minefield of motion sensors and high-definition cameras. To walk across the lobby was to invite a prison sentence.

"The lift," Basil gestured.

They took the elevator to the second floor, the mechanical groan of the motor sounding like a roar in the empty building. When the doors slid open, they didn't exit into the hallway. Instead, they jammed the mechanism, forcing the heavy metal doors to stay open.

Danny peered over the edge into the **elevator shaft**. It was a vertical tunnel of oily darkness, stretching down into the bowels of the basement. This was the "dead zone," a path invisible to every camera in the building.

One by one, the elderly thieves buckled into harnesses. They didn't have the speed of youth, but they had the steadiness of men who had nothing left to lose. They **abseiled down the lift shaft**, sliding down the thick, greasy cables like spiders descending into a web. Their boots touched the basement floor with a soft thud, far beneath the reach of the sensors upstairs.

They stood before the final obstacle: the vault wall. It was **50cm of reinforced concrete**, a massive gray slab that stood between them and £14 million in diamonds and gold.

Danny Jones stepped forward, hauling the **Hilti DD350**. This was the weapon he had researched for three long years. He bolted the heavy rig to the floor, the metallic clinks echoing off the basement walls. He checked the water-cooling line and adjusted the diamond-tipped bit.

"Do it," Perkins grunted.

Danny pulled the trigger. The drill roared to life, a high-pitched mechanical scream that vibrated through the very foundation of Hatton Garden. Sparks didn't fly; instead, a gray slurry of wet concrete dust began to ooze from the wall as the diamond teeth bit deep.

For hours, they worked in the sweltering, dust-choked basement. They weren't just drilling a hole;

they were performing a mechanical autopsy. Danny aimed for precision, boring **three large, overlapping holes**. He needed to create a passage wide enough for a man to crawl through, a bridge between the world of the ordinary and the world of the unimaginable.

As the third hole neared completion, the concrete began to groan. The "Grandfathers" stood back, sweat dripping from their brows, watching as the final block of the 50cm wall trembled. They had bypassed the keys, killed the alarms, conquered the abyss of the lift shaft, and now, the fortress itself was beginning to crack.

The drill bit finally punched through into the hollow space of the vault. The thieves knew the hardest part was supposedly over, but as the dust settled, they had no idea that an unexpected variable on the other side of that hole was about to turn their "perfect" plan into a nightmare.

Obstacles

The basement of 88–90 Hatton Garden was a tomb of gray dust and mechanical heat. The air was so thick with the pulverized remains of 50cm-thick reinforced concrete that the beams from the gang's headlamps looked like solid swords of light cutting through a fog.

For hours, the high-pitched shriek of the **Hilti DD350** had been the only heartbeat in the room. Danny Jones, his face coated in a mask of white slurry, felt the vibration die down as the diamond-tipped bit finally spun into empty air. The three overlapping holes were complete. They had successfully bored a jagged, circular window through the fortress wall.

"We're in," Danny whispered, his voice cracking from the dust.

But as the dust settled, the victory felt wrong. Terry Perkins stepped forward, shining his heavy industrial torch through the new opening. He didn't see the glint of gold or the sparkling reflections of thousands of diamonds. Instead, the light hit a flat, dull surface of heavy-gauge blue steel.

On the other side of their meticulously drilled hole sat a **massive metal storage cabinet**. It wasn't just sitting there; it was a monolith, bolted firmly into the floor and the ceiling of the vault. It acted as a secondary skin, a metal shield that their drill couldn't reach and their crowbars couldn't budge.

"You've got to be kidding me," Perkins hissed, his hand slamming against the concrete.

They took turns pressing their shoulders into the gap, trying to heave the cabinet forward. The metal didn't even groan. It was an immovable object met by an exhausted force. The "Grandfathers" were strong, but they were also men in their 60s and 70s, and the physical toll of the night was beginning to show.

As they wrestled with the cabinet, a tiny red light on a panel near the ceiling began to pulse. They had been careful, they had cut the telephone lines, but the vault had secrets they hadn't fully mapped.

At **12:21 am on Friday, April 3rd**, the silence of the basement was shattered by the internal realization that an alarm had been triggered.

"Quiet!" Reader commanded.

They froze. Every breath was a risk. Above them, in the world of the living, a signal had reached a monitoring station. The "gag" they had placed on the building's phone lines had a fail-safe, or perhaps a local vibration sensor had finally had enough.

Minutes felt like hours. Then, the sound they dreaded most: the crunch of tires on the gravel outside the side entrance. A security guard had arrived.

Inside the basement, the thieves were trapped. They couldn't go up the lift shaft without being heard, and they couldn't stay if the police were coming. They huddled in the shadows of the machinery, their hearts hammering against their ribs like trapped birds.

Outside, the security guard stepped out of his vehicle. He walked to the side door—the very door Basil had opened with a stolen key hours earlier. He rattled the handle. He shone his flashlight through the glass.

But the thieves had been meticulous. There were no signs of forced entry on the exterior. Because of a massive underground fire nearby that had been causing electrical glitches across London all night, the guard was skeptical of the alarm. He looked at the door, saw it was locked, and made a fateful decision.

He got back in his car and drove away.

The relief in the basement was thick enough to taste, but it was followed by a cold realization: they were stuck.

"We can't get past it," Danny said, staring at the blue metal cabinet through the hole. "Not with what we've got here."

The gang stood in a circle, the dust settling on their shoulders like snow. Brian Reader, the Mastermind, looked at the hole and then at his watch. The sun would be up soon. The Friday morning traffic would begin. The risk of staying was becoming astronomical.

"We leave," Reader said firmly.

"Leave?" Perkins' voice rose in a raspy growl. "We've spent three years on this!"

"We leave, we regroup, and we come back with something that can move mountains," Reader replied, his eyes cold.

They began the grueling process of the retreat. They hauled their heavy bags back to the elevator shaft. One by one, they climbed back up the greasy cables, their muscles screaming in protest. They slipped out the side door just as the first grey light of Friday morning began to bleed into the London sky.

As they piled into the van, the silence was heavy. They had the hole, but they didn't have the prize.

"What now?" Collins asked from the driver's seat.

Danny Jones looked at his hands, still vibrating from the drill. "We need a **10-ton hydraulic ram**," he said. "And we're coming back tomorrow night to finish this".

The van pulled away, a ghost in the morning fog, leaving the vault behind—for now. Little did they know, the police were already beginning to look for a **white Mercedes** that had been seen one too many times in the Garden.

The Return of the Ram

London, Saturday, April 4th, The air was thick with the scent of rain and city exhaust, but for the "Grandfathers," the only smell that mattered was the metallic tang of defeat they had tasted the night before. They were back at the side door of 88–90 Hatton Garden, but the atmosphere had changed. The group was smaller. Brian Reader, the "Mastermind," had looked at the odds and the massive metal cabinet blocking their path and decided he was out. He had walked away, leaving the others to finish what they had started three years ago.

Danny Jones, Terry Perkins, and John "Kenny" Collins stood in the shadows, their breath hitching in the cold air. They weren't just thieves anymore; they were men on a mission to reclaim their pride.

They entered the building exactly as they had before, a repeat performance of a dark ballet. Basil, the man in the red wig, led the way through the side door. They abseiled down the lift shaft once more, their gloved hands gripping the greasy cables with a new, desperate strength.

When they reached the basement, the jagged holes they had bored into the 50cm-thick concrete wall looked like a taunt. Beyond those holes sat the blue metal cabinet—the immovable object.

"Bring it forward," Danny Jones grunted.

They hauled the **10-ton hydraulic ram** into position. It was a heavy, yellow piece of industrial machinery, a squat beast designed to exert enough pressure to crush a car. They wedged the base of the ram against the back of the vault wall and aligned the piston with the metal cabinet through the hole.

The sound of the manual pump was a rhythmic *thwack-hiss* that filled the cramped basement. Danny Jones pumped the handle, his muscles burning. For a long minute, nothing happened. The metal cabinet seemed to absorb the pressure, silent and stubborn. Then, a sound like a gunshot echoed through the vault.

A bolt had snapped.

The cabinet groaned a deep, metallic scream of protesting steel. Danny kept pumping. Slowly, inch by agonizing inch, the massive cabinet began to tilt, its anchors tearing out of the ceiling with the sound of cracking stone. Finally, with a thunderous crash that shook the floor, the cabinet was shoved aside.

The path was clear.

Terry Perkins was the first to scramble through the hole. He emerged into the vault, his flashlight beam dancing across rows upon rows of steel safe deposit boxes. It was a cathedral of wealth, silent and cold.

They didn't have much time. They knew the clock was ticking toward morning. Working with frantic energy, they used angle grinders and crowbars to tear into the boxes. Sparks rained down as the grinders bit into the steel locks. One box after another gave way, spilling its contents into the dust.

It was a chaotic treasure hunt. They found velvet pouches overflowing with loose diamonds that shimmered like ice in their headlamps. There were heavy bars of solid gold, stacks of British pounds, and rare watches that cost more than a suburban house.

"Look at this!" Perkins hissed, holding up a handful of emeralds.

They didn't celebrate. They stuffed the loot into ordinary wheelie bins and laundry bags. They were loading **£14 million** in stolen wealth into the same bins people used for their weekly trash. By the time the first light of Sunday, April 5th, hit the streets of London, they were gone.

The Flying Squad

April 7th, 8am. Kelvin Stockwell, a veteran security guard, was among the first to arrive at the building that morning. He had spent years walking these halls, and he knew the building's quirks—the way the floors creaked, the hum of the old elevator. But as he stepped through the side entrance, his internal alarm began to blare.

The building was too quiet. The air felt heavy, as if it were holding its breath.

Stockwell made his way toward the elevator. When he reached the second floor, his heart skipped a beat. The elevator doors were jammed wide open, the car nowhere to be seen. He leaned over the threshold, peering into the vertical abyss of the lift shaft. A tangle of greasy cables and shadows greeted him.

"What on earth..." he whispered, his voice disappearing into the darkness.

He descended to the basement, his footsteps echoing like gunshots against the tile. The smell hit him first—the unmistakable, chalky scent of pulverized concrete and the scorched-metal aroma of an angle grinder. As he turned the corner toward the vault, the sight before him froze the blood in his veins.

The vault's outer gate was intact, but the 50cm-thick reinforced concrete wall looked like it had been hit by a wrecking ball. Three jagged, overlapping circular holes had been bored straight through the stone. Through the breach, he could see the carnage: the massive blue storage cabinet, once bolted to the floor, lay crumpled like a discarded tin can.

Beyond the hole, the vault was a disaster zone. Safe deposit boxes had been ripped from the walls and cast aside like empty candy wrappers. Diamonds, gold dust, and discarded velvet pouches littered the floor.

Stockwell didn't call for a locksmith. He didn't call the building manager. He reached for his radio with trembling fingers.

"We've been breached," he croaked into the receiver. "The vault... it's gone. It's all gone."

By mid-morning, the quiet street of Hatton Garden was transformed into a sea of blue lights and yellow crime-scene tape. The **Flying Squad**, the Metropolitan Police's elite unit specializing in high-stakes robberies, had taken over the scene.

Detective Chief Inspector (DCI) Paul Johnson stepped out of his car, his eyes scanning the building's exterior. He was joined by Detective Superintendent Craig Turner. They were men who had seen every type of heist imaginable, from bank heists to armored car robberies, but they knew Hatton Garden was a different beast entirely.

"The alarm logs say it triggered Friday at 00:21," Turner said, checking his notes as they walked toward the basement. "We didn't send a car. Thought it was a false positive from the fire in Holborn."

Johnson jaw tightened. "That's going to bite us in the ass, Craig. Let's see what they left us."

As they entered the basement, both men stopped. The scale of the operation was staggering.

"This wasn't a smash-and-grab," Johnson said, his voice hushed with a grudging respect as he inspected the holes in the wall. "This was a siege. Look at the precision of these cuts. They used a core drill. They knew exactly where the rebar was."

Turner pointed to a heavy piece of machinery abandoned near the breach—the **Hilti DD350**. "They left the drill. And the hydraulic ram."

"They left them because they couldn't carry them back up the shaft with £14 million in diamonds on their backs," Johnson replied. "Start the forensic sweep. I want every millimeter of this basement dusted. Check the water in the cooling tanks—maybe they left DNA. Check the lift cables. They abseiled down, so they must have left some sign of their gear."

The investigation moved with the agonizing slowness of a forensic autopsy. Crime Scene Investigators in white Tyvek suits crawled through the dust. They used laser scanners to map the opening left by the drill and tweezers to pick up tiny flecks of blue paint from the storage cabinet.

"Sir," a CSI called out, gesturing to the floor inside the vault. "We've got something. Not much, but something."

Johnson and Turner stepped carefully through the hole. On the floor lay a series of discarded tools: crowbars, angle grinders, and a pile of shattered safe deposit box doors.

"They smashed 73 boxes," Turner noted, looking at the devastation. "They were selective. They didn't just take everything; they knew which ones were worth the weight."

"Look at the phone lines," Johnson said, pointing to a severed cluster of wires near the ceiling. "Clean snips. They knew the layout. They knew where the eyes were."

"It's an old-school job, Paul," Turner remarked. "Heavy thieving."

"Old school or not, they're ghosts," Johnson said, looking at the dust-covered floor. "No prints. No DNA so far. They wore gloves, masks, the works. If we're going to catch them, we have to look outside these walls."

By the morning of April 8th, the investigation had shifted from the basement to the "War Room" at the Flying Squad's headquarters. The strategy was simple but monumental: find the vehicles.

"They didn't walk home with wheelie bins full of gold," Johnson told his team. "I want every scrap of CCTV from every camera within a two-mile radius of Hatton Garden. I want it from Thursday night, Friday morning, Saturday night, and Sunday morning."

Detectives began the grueling task of reviewing thousands of hours of grainy footage. They weren't just looking for the heist weekend; they were looking for the **reconnaissance phase**.

"If they planned this for years, they were here before," Turner said, leaning over a technician's shoulder. "They had to be. Nobody drills three overlapping holes through 50cm of concrete by guessing where the vault is."

Late that afternoon, a breakthrough flickered on a screen.

"Boss, look at this," a young detective called out. "We've got a white van moving toward the side entrance on Thursday night. But look what's following it a few minutes later."

On the screen, a **white Mercedes E200** with distinctive, darkened alloy rims cruised slowly past the building. It didn't belong to a jeweler. It didn't belong to a resident.

"That's a scout car," Johnson said, his eyes narrowing. "Run the plate through the ANPR (Automatic Number Plate Recognition). See where that car was on Friday and Saturday. And more importantly, see where it was six months ago."

Turner runs the plate and after some time the computer screen flickers with and address and a name. Turner replies, "Plate comes back to a John

Collins. He's got a record as long as your arm, Paul. Mostly heavy thieving. But he's 74 years old."

Johnson reads the information on the screen intently saying, "A 74-year-old abseiling down a lift shaft? Not likely. He's the driver. If Collins is involved, he's not alone. Who does he talk to? Who are his contemporaries?"

Turner jots down a phone number and hands it to an assistant, "We're checking his phone records now. If he was in the Garden that night, his cell phone might have pinged a tower, even if he didn't make a call."

Johnson shakes his head skeptically, "They're smart, Craig. They probably used 'burners' or walkie-talkies during the job. But they're old. They'll get sloppy when they think they've won. They'll start talking. They'll go to their usual pubs. They'll want to celebrate."

"You think it's the 'Old Guard'?" Turner asks.

"I think we're looking for a group of grandfathers who just pulled off the heist of the century. And they're currently sitting somewhere with £14 million worth of diamonds, trying to figure out how to melt down the gold without us hearing the furnace." Johnson says, as he walks away.

By the end of April 8th, the Flying Squad had established their beachhead. They had the drill, the forensic map of the breach, and the first "thread"— the white Mercedes.

The investigation was no longer about a hole in a wall; it was a digital hunt across the cellular networks and CCTV grids of London. The thieves had escaped the building, but they had left a ghost in the machine. The Flying Squad was beginning to close the distance, moving from the physical dust of the basement to the invisible signals of the city.

The hunt for the Hatton Garden "Grandfathers" had truly begun.

The Invisible Net

The investigation into the Hatton Garden heist shifted from the dusty, silent basement of the vault to the high-tech, neon-lit "War Room" of the Metropolitan Police's Flying Squad. The hunt was no longer about concrete and drills; it was about signals, shadows, and the arrogance of men who thought they were untouchable.

Detective Chief Inspector (DCI) Paul Johnson stood before a massive digital map of London, his eyes tracking a series of red dots that represented the movement of a single vehicle: the **white Mercedes E200**.

"The ANPR (Automatic Number Plate Recognition) hits are consistent," Detective Superintendent Craig Turner said, tapping a tablet. "This car was circling Hatton Garden for months before the heist. And it was there on the night of the second breach."

"And the owner?" Johnson asked.

"John 'Kenny' Collins," Turner replied. "Seventy-four years old. He's been in the game since the sixties. He's our thread."

The detectives began a process known as **Call Data Mapping**. They pulled the records for Collins' personal mobile phone. While the gang had likely used walkie-talkies or "burner" phones during the actual heist to stay off the grid, they had been less careful during the three years of planning.

"He's calling three main numbers," a digital forensic analyst reported. "One belongs to Terry Perkins—another veteran, age sixty-seven. Another to Daniel Jones, age fifty-eight. And the third... it's a landline for a Brian Reader, age seventy-six."

Johnson leaned back, a grim smile on his face. "The 'Grandfathers.' They aren't just a crew; they're the 'Old Guard' of the London underworld. They think we've forgotten them because they've been 'retired.' They think we're only looking for kids with laptops."

The investigation moved from the digital world to the physical one. The phone records showed a pattern: the men were meeting regularly at a pub in Islington called **The Castle**.

The Flying Squad launched a high-stakes surveillance operation. They couldn't just walk in with badges; these thieves were "hyper-aware." They knew how to spot a tail, and they knew what a police officer looked like, even in plain clothes.

Undercover officers (UCs) were deployed, posing as local workmen, hipsters, and regulars.

They wore hidden cameras and microphones, but the pub was noisy, filled with the clatter of glasses and the roar of football matches on the TV.

"Target one (Collins) and Target two (Perkins) are at the corner booth. They're leaning in close. I can't hear a word over the racket in this place." One of the undercovers complains into a mic hidden in his collar.

Detective Johnson responds from a remote command center a couple of blocks away, "Stay patient. Don't get too close. We don't need to hear them yet—we just need to see who they're meeting."

"Wait... a man just walked in. Red hair. Cap pulled low." The UC says as he draws a drink to his lips.

"That may be the Infiltrator. Keep the eyes on him. He's the ghost." Johnson says with intensity in his voice.

To bypass the noise of the pub, the police brought in a specialist tool: **professional lip-readers**. From across the street, using high-powered binoculars and long-range lenses, undercover officers watched the gang's mouths. They "heard" the thieves talking about "the diamonds," "the furnace," and "the weight of the gold."

The UCs had identified the players, but they still didn't have the loot. To find the £14 million in diamonds and gold, they needed to hear the "Grandfathers" when they thought they were truly alone.

In the dead of night, technical specialists from the Flying Squad performed a "black-bag job". They broke into John Collins' white Mercedes and Terry Perkins' Citroen Berlingo van. They didn't steal anything; instead, they planted **highly sensitive audio bugs** deep within the upholstery and the dashboards.

Now, the Flying Squad was riding shotgun.

After several hours of staking out two elderly gentlemen approach the Mercedes and get in. Detectives prepare recording devices as the vehicle begins to the pull away, they pull away as well to follow.

"We've done it, Kenny. The biggest robbery in the world. We're legends. Those kids today... they couldn't even find the basement, let alone drill through it." Perkins says excitedly starting the conversation.

"We still need to move the 'sparklers' (diamonds). The gold is easy—we melt that down— but the stones leave a trail." Collins complains.

Perkins shakes his head dismissively, "Don't worry about it. This is our pension. I'm going to buy a place where the sun never stops shining. I can almost taste the champagne."

The police listened at the sheer arrogance of the men. Perkins was recorded boasting about how he had "pissed himself" with excitement when they finally broke into the vault. They were mocking the police, unaware that every boast was being recorded and transcribed several yards away.

The most chilling revelation came from Daniel Jones. The bugs picked up a conversation about the safety of their "retirement fund." Officers staking out he van location recorded Jones saying, "I've put mine where the dead don't talk," The detectives analyzed the GPS data from Jones' phone and his car. They tracked him to **Edmonton Cemetery** in north London. Under the cover of darkness, undercover officers watched as Jones wandered among the tombstones, stopping at a specific memorial stone. He wasn't mourning; he was checking his bank account.

"He's buried it," Johnson whispered, watching the grainy thermal footage. "He's buried the loot in a graveyard."

Operation Overlark

By mid-May, the Flying Squad had enough evidence to convict the gang ten times over. They had the recordings, the CCTV, the lip-read transcripts, and the locations of several stashes. But they were waiting for the "Handover"—the moment the gang gathered to split the final portion of the loot.

"We move tomorrow," Johnson announced to a room of 200 officers on the evening of May 18th. "They're meeting to move the jewelry. If we don't hit them now, those diamonds disappear into the black market, and we'll never see them again."

The plan was codenamed **Operation Overlark**. It was to be a simultaneous strike across

12 different addresses to ensure no one could tip off the others.

Turner raised his hand and asked, "What about 'Basil'? We still don't have a real name for him."

"We'll take the ones we have. The 'Grandfathers' are the heart of this. Once they're in cuffs, the ghost will have nowhere to hide." Johnson replies confidently.

At dawn on May 19th, the silence of a dozen London streets was shattered by the sound of battering rams.

The "Grandfathers" were caught completely off guard. Terry Perkins was arrested in his pajamas, surrounded by bags of jewelry. John Collins was pulled from his bed, his "scout car" parked outside, now a piece of evidence.

When they reached Daniel Jones, the man who had researched the Hilti drill for three years, he looked at Detective Johnson and realized the game was over.

"You lot were busy, weren't you?" Jones reportedly said, a smirk still playing on his lips even as the handcuffs clicked shut.

The "Old Guard" had been outmaneuvered not by a faster drill, but by an invisible net of digital signals and silent observers. The heist of the century had ended not in a getaway to a sun-drenched beach, but in the back of a police van, headed for the cold reality of a prison cell.

The Trial and the Reckoning

The final act of the Hatton Garden heist didn't take place in a dark vault or a smoky pub, but in the sterile, high-ceilinged rooms of the **Woolwich Crown Court**. The "Grandfathers" had traded their high-visibility vests for cheap suits, and the swagger they once had in Terry Perkins' Citroen Berlingo had evaporated under the harsh glare of the judicial system.

This was the end of the line.

November 2015 – January 2016. The trial was a media circus. People were fascinated by the "Old School" nature of the crime—a group of pensioners using a 10-ton ram to pull off a multi-million-pound heist in the age of cybersecurity. But for the victims—the jewelers whose livelihoods had been stuffed into wheelie bins—there was nothing charming about it.

Detective Paul Johnson and his team from the Flying Squad sat in the gallery, watching as the evidence they had painstakingly gathered was presented to the jury.

"Mr. Perkins, we have hours of recordings of you boasting about this being your 'pension.' You even mocked the police for missing the alarm. Do you still find the situation as humorous as you did in your car?" The Prosecutor asks rhetorically.

Perkins sits silently staring down at his hands.

The Prosecutor continues, "And Mr. Jones, you led the police to a cemetery. You pretended to be helpful by showing us two bags of loot, all while hiding a third bag just a few feet away. Was that part of the 'meticulous planning' we've heard so much about?"

The evidence was overwhelming. The prosecution played the "Bragging Tapes" captured by the car bugs. The jury heard the thieves laughing about the heist and arguing over how to split the diamonds. They saw the CCTV of the white Mercedes scouting the building. They saw the Hilti drill, still caked in the concrete dust of the vault.

In March 2016, the judge handed down the sentences.

- **John "Kenny" Collins (75), Daniel Jones (60), and Terry Perkins (67)** were each sentenced to **seven years** in prison.
- **Brian Reader (77)**, the "Mastermind" who had walked away before the second night, received **six years and three months**.
- Other accomplices who helped move the loot received varying sentences based on their involvement.

But the legal battle wasn't over. Under the **Proceeds of Crime Act**, the government demanded that the men pay back the millions of pounds that were still missing.

"You claim the loot is gone," the judge remarked during a later hearing. "But the math doesn't add up. There is still roughly **£4 million to £7 million** unaccounted for. If you do not pay, you will stay in prison."

Because they couldn't (or wouldn't) produce the missing millions, Collins, Jones, and Perkins were handed **extra "default" sentences of seven years each**. For men of their age, this was essentially... A life sentence.

One question haunted the Flying Squad For three years:

Who was "Basil"?

The man in the red wig, the one with the keys, had vanished into thin air the morning of the heist. He had only been at the pub once; he hadn't been in the bugged cars. He was the ultimate ghost.

But in March 2018, the ghost finally materialized. Following a fresh tip and years of cold-case work, police raided a flat in Islington. There, they found **Michael Seed**, a 57-year-old alarm specialist and jeweler.

Inside his apartment, detectives found a professional gold-melting furnace and **£143,000 worth of jewelry** and gold ingots hidden in his bedroom. Forensic analysis of the Hatton Garden CCTV confirmed that Seed's gait and height matched "Basil" perfectly. In 2019, he was sentenced to **ten years** in prison, finally closing the book on the gang members.

Despite the arrests and the recovery of several stashes (including the cemetery bags), a significant portion of the **£14 million** haul was never found.

- **The Melt-Down:** Police believe much of the gold was quickly melted down into untraceable bars and sold through shady dealers in the days immediately following the heist.
- **The Black Market:** The highest-quality diamonds were likely smuggled out of the country, destined for private collections in Europe or Asia where they could never be identified.
- **The Secret Stashes:** To this day, rumors persist that more bags of jewelry are buried in parks or cemeteries across London, waiting for a day that will never come for the men who put them there.

The Last of the Old School

The Hatton Garden heist was more than just a robbery; it was the end of an era.

Terry Perkins died in prison in 2018, just days after being ordered to pay back the missing millions. **Brian Reader** was released early due to failing health, a shadow of the man who had once been the most feared name in the London underworld.

Detective Paul Johnson, now retired, often reflects on the case. "They were clever, and they were patient," he once said in an interview. "But they were arrogant. They thought the world had stopped moving in 1980. They learned how to use a drill from

YouTube, but they forgot that YouTube works both ways. The digital world they used to plan the job was the same world we used to catch them."

The hole in the vault wall has long since been repaired. The safety deposit boxes have been replaced. But in the quiet hours of the night in Hatton Garden, you can still hear the echoes of the "Grandfathers"—the screech of a diamond drill, the groan of a hydraulic ram, and the fading laughter of men who thought they had finally won their pension, only to find they had bought themselves a cage.

Sources

- BBC News. "Hatton Garden Heist: 'The Last of the Old-school Raiders'." January 14, 2016. https://www.bbc.com/news/uk-35293649.
- BBC News. "Hatton Garden Heist: Police 'Let Down' Victims." June 15, 2015. https://www.bbc.com/news/uk-33104523.
- Catt's True Crime Corner. "The Hatton Garden Heist." March 24, 2018. https://catts-true-crime-corner.com/the-hatton-garden-heist/.
- Hilti Group. "Diamond Core Drilling Machine DD 350-CA." Accessed June 2024. https://www.hilti.co.uk/c/CLS_POWER_TOOLS_7124/CLS_DIAMOND_CORING_7124/CLS_DIAMOND_CORE_RIGS_7124/r4700.
- The Daily Mail. "Mastermind of the Hatton Garden Heist: Brian Reader Sentenced." January 14, 2016. https://www.dailymail.co.uk/news/article-3401037/Mastermind-Hatton-Garden-heist-Brian-Reader-sentenced.html.
- The Guardian. "Hatton Garden Safe Deposit Raid: Police Arrest Nine Suspects." May 19, 2015. https://www.theguardian.com/uk-news/2015/may/19/hatton-garden-safe-deposit-raid-police-arrest-nine-suspects.
- The Independent. "Hatton Garden Heist: The Target, The Plan, The Job, The Gear and The Investigation." January 14, 2016. https://www.independent.co.uk/news/uk/crime/hatton-garden-heist-the-target-the-plan-the-job-the-gear-and-the-investigation-a6812321.html.

- Kustom Signals. "How Police Solved The Biggest Diamond Heist In History." October 16, 2019. https://kustomsignals.com/blog/how-police-solved-the-biggest-diamond-heist-in-history/.
- Sky News. "Hatton Garden Heist: How The Gang Was Caught." January 14, 2016. https://news.sky.com/story/hatton-garden-heist-how-the-gang-was-caught-10130635.
- VOA News. "Prosecutors: Easter Jewel Heist Was Largest in English History." November 23, 2015. https://www.voanews.com/a/prosecutors-easter-jewel-heist-was-largest-in-english-history/3070381.html.
- Wikipedia. "Hatton Garden Safe Deposit Burglary." Accessed June 2024. https://en.wikipedia.org/wiki/Hatton_Garden_safe_deposit_burglary.

Harry Winston Heist: A Pink Panther Caper

The Fortress of Luxury

The air on Avenue Montaigne was crisp, a mix, smelling of expensive perfume, the exhaust of idling Mercedes and Bentleys and the impending December chill. Avenue Montaigne is a broad, tree-lined boulevard that connects the Champs-Élysées to the Place de l'Alma, this is a place where the sidewalks are scrubbed clean almost daily.

In December, the street is a spectacle of high-end holiday decor. It was the height of the Christmas shopping season. The sidewalk was crowded with wealthy tourists, high-society Parisians, and "window-shoppers" peering at displays behind reinforced glass.

Because the street holds billions of dollars in inventory, it is one of the most heavily surveilled stretches of pavement in the world. Private security guards in dark suits stood outside almost every door. Plainclothes police officers from the local precinct often patrolled the area, looking for pickpockets or "spotters."

Unlike a department store, Harry Winston was a fortress. You didn't just walk in; you were viewed through a camera and "buzzed" through a double-set of security doors (a "man-trap" system).

The December wind whipped down Avenue Montaigne, cutting right through the expensive wool coat and biting at the nylon stockings Douadi Yahiaoui wore. He stood near the polished glass display of the Loewe boutique, fifty feet from the target. To the passing world—the tourists bundled in scarves, the Parisian socialites stepping out of black sedans—he was just another wealthy blonde woman contemplating a five-thousand-euro handbag. But beneath the itchy synthetic wig and the layers of silk, sweat was already trickling down his ribs. The disguise was impeccable, a necessary humiliation to bypass the first layer of security, but every second spent teetering in the unfamiliar high heels felt like an eternity exposed on a stage.

Beside him, the youngest member of the crew, also dressed as a woman, was fidgeting. He kept adjusting the collar of his fur coat, his eyes darting too quickly toward the armed private security guard pacing in front of the Dior store across the street. The tension in the young man's posture was a beacon that could blow the whole operation before it began. Yahiaoui stepped closer, feigning an interest in a leather tote bag in the window, leaning in so their shoulders touched.

"Quit twitching," Yahiaoui hissed under his breath, forcing a stiff smile for anyone watching. "You're not a thief right now. You're a bored housewife spending her husband's bonus. Fix your posture. Look arrogant, not scared."

The younger man stiffened, forced a nod, and tilted his chin up, channeling the disdainful air of the neighborhood's regular clientele. "It's the guard," he whispered back, barely moving his painted lips. "He's looking right at us."

"He's looking at your ass in that skirt," Yahiaoui snapped quietly. "Let him look. We're waiting for the right moment. Trust the timing." He glanced at his watch—a delicate Cartier knockoff that looked real enough from a distance. 5:28 PM. They needed the sidewalk traffic to thicken just enough to provide a visual shield, a moment of chaotic normalcy to cover their transition from shoppers to raiders.

Then, the rhythm of the street shifted. A small tour bus emptied a dozen noisy patrons near the Plaza Athénée, and simultaneously, a large delivery truck rumbled past, momentarily blocking the view from the opposite sidewalk. It was the seam in the universe they had been waiting for. Yahiaoui felt the familiar surge of adrenaline, sharper and colder than the winter air. He gave the slightest nod to the fourth man—the only one dressed in male clothing, acting as their escort.

"Showtime," Yahiaoui murmured. The four of them turned away from the safety of the Loewe window. They began the thirty-foot walk toward Number 29, their heels clicking on the pavement like a countdown clock. Yahiaoui fixed his eyes on the camera lens above the Harry Winston door, composing his face into a mask of entitled boredom, praying the buzzer would sound before his heart hammered right out of his chest.

Yahiaoui pushes the buzzer for entry. A security guard glanced at the monitor. He saw three elegant women—blonde, draped in fashionable coats, balancing on high heels—and a male companion. He pressed the button. The magnetic lock clicked open.

As the door swung shut, the "women" didn't head for the engagement rings. They moved with a sudden, jarring masculinity. Douadi Yahiaoui, reached into a designer handbag. He didn't pull out a credit card; he pulled out a .357 Magnum. Another man brandished a smooth, olive-drab hand grenade.

"Nobody moves," Yahiaoui barked. The feminine wig sat slightly askew on his head, a grotesque contrast to the cold steel in his hand.

There were fifteen people in the store—a mix of wealthy clients and veteran staff. Panic began to rise, but it was instantly stifled by a chilling detail.

"Don't be a hero, **Mickaël**," one of the gunmen hissed, pointing his weapon directly at a trembling floor manager.

The staff froze. *How did they know his name?* The thieves moved through the room, addressing employees by their first names as if they were old friends. This wasn't a random hit; this was an execution of a plan fueled by an "Inside Man".

"Get them in the corner! Move!" the third thief shouted, herding the victims into a tight group near the back. "Hands where I can see them. If one person screams, we drop the grenade. Do you understand?"

The thieves didn't waste time on the display cases near the windows. They knew the layout better than the customers did.

"The safes," Yahiaoui commanded, gesturing toward the back offices. "The ones you think we don't know about. Open them. Now."

One of the managers fumbled with the keys, his hands shaking so violently they rattled against the metal. "Faster," the gunman whispered, the barrel of the Magnum pressing into the man's temple. "We're on the clock."

The heavy doors groaned open. Inside lay the "private collection"—pieces destined for royalty and movie stars. The thieves began sweeping the jewels into large, unassuming bags. Necklaces that could buy a fleet of yachts were stuffed in like laundry.

While the leader cleared the safes, the others turned back to the showroom. *CRACK*. The sound of a sledgehammer meeting reinforced glass echoed like a gunshot. They weren't surgical; they were efficient. They prioritized the "Big Rocks"—the high-carat diamonds that were easy to transport and hard to trace once pried from their settings.

"Is that all of it?" one thief shouted over the sound of breaking glass. "We have the storage units," Yahiaoui replied, hoisting a bag heavy with gold and platinum. "Let's go. Time's up."

The heist had taken less than twenty minutes. The gunmen didn't run out the door screaming; they walked out with the same chilling confidence they had entered with.

"Stay on the floor for five minutes," Yahiaoui warned the victims. "If I see a face at that window, the grenade comes back through the glass."

They stepped out into the Paris evening. A nondescript getaway car was idling at the curb. By the time the first police siren wailed in the distance, the "women" in the blonde wigs had vanished into the labyrinth of Paris traffic, carrying $100 million in diamonds and leaving behind a room full of people who were too terrified to even breathe.

The Pink Panthers

The roar of the getaway car faded into the hum of the Paris evening, leaving the Avenue Montaigne in a state of shattered silence. Inside the boutique, the air was thick with the smell of ozone from broken electronics and the metallic tang of fear. It took exactly three minutes for the first "Police Nationale" sirens to scream onto the boulevard. Within ten minutes, the "Golden Triangle" was cordoned off with yellow tape, the flickering blue lights reflecting off the diamonds left behind in the debris.

Leading the charge was the **Brigade de Répression du Banditisme (BRB)**, France's elite anti-gang unit. **Chief Inspector Patrick Visser** stepped over the threshold, his boots crunching on a fragment of a $200,000 display case. He didn't look at the jewelry; he looked at the staff. They were huddled together, some weeping, others staring blankly at the walls.

"Talk to me," Visser commanded, his voice a low gravel. "Tell me they didn't just walk out the front door."

A forensic technician, already dusting the glass for prints he knew he wouldn't find, looked up. "They just walk out, Chief. They vanished. No shots fired, no alarms tripped until they were already in the car. It was efficient and calculated."

Visser approached the store manager, who was being wrapped in a shock blanket. "The names," Visser said, his tone softening but urgent. "We heard they called you by your names. Is that true?"

The manager nodded, his teeth chattering. "They knew... they knew Mickaël was the one with the keys to the back safe. They knew I had just come back from lunch. They knew everything, Monsieur. It was like they lived here."

Visser's eyes narrowed as he looked at the security team standing near the door. The suspicion was immediate. "They had a roadmap," he muttered to his deputy. "This wasn't just luck. This was a script provided by someone on the payroll."

Back at the BRB headquarters on Quai des Orfèvres, the phones were already melting. The scale of the theft—nearly $100 million—had reached the highest levels of the French government. The pressure was immense. By midnight, the dossier was dubbed "The Heist of the Century." Visser sat in a dark office, staring at the grainiest CCTV footage he had ever seen. The blonde wigs looked like ghosts on the screen.

"It's the Panthers," his deputy said, dropping a folder onto the desk. "The MO fits. The Balkan connection. The speed. The 'disguises as theater' tactic. Interpol is already flagging similar hits in London and Tokyo."

"Maybe," Visser replied, lighting a cigarette despite there being a "NO SMOKING" sign on the wall directly above the computer screen.. "But the Panthers usually hit and run. This crew... they were comfortable. They spent twenty minutes inside. That's an eternity in a heist. They knew the police response time to the second. They knew which safes were dummy units and which ones held the Graff diamonds. Someone gave them the keys to the kingdom," he told a junior officer. "And until we find that person, those diamonds are already being broken down in a basement in Belgrade."

The investigation began with a brutal, systematic sweep of every employee's life. Visser spent the next forty-eight hours in an interrogation room, his eyes bloodshot. He wasn't looking for a master criminal; he was looking for a leak.

The fluorescent lights of the BRB briefing room hummed with a sterile, electric tension. A thick haze of cigarette smoke hung over a folding table cluttered with grainy photos of the Harry Winston crime scene and blurred surveillance stills from three continents. Chief Inspector Visser leaned against the back wall, arms crossed, his gaze fixed on the man standing at the head of the room—**Agent Stefan Novak**, a senior operative from Interpol's specialized "Project Pink Panther" task force.

Novak clicked a remote, and the projector flared to life, casting the image of a blue diamond ring submerged in a jar of expensive face cream. "This is where the myth began," Novak started, his voice carrying the jagged edge of a Belgrade accent. "London, 2003. Graff Diamonds. Our suspects hid a three-quarter-million-dollar stone in a pot of cold cream, just like a scene from the 1975 Peter Sellers film. The British press gave them the name "Pink

Panthers", and unfortunately, the gang has spent the last five years living up to the Hollywood theatrics."

A junior detective scuffs, leaning forward into the light. "We're dealing with movie buffs? Is that the profile?"

"Don't let the name fool you into thinking they're a joke," Novak snapped, clicking to the next slide. It wasn't a jewelry store; it was a grainy photo of soldiers in camouflage standing over a scorched landscape. "These aren't petty thieves. They are the leftovers of the Yugoslav Wars. Veterans of the Serbian Special Forces and paramilitary units from Montenegro and Croatia. When the sanctions hit and the industries collapsed, they took the only skills they had—tactical entry, surveillance, and ballistics—and took them to the private sector."

Visser stepped into the light, his face shadowed. "Explain the structure, Novak. We're looking for a kingpin. A 'Big Boss' we can squeeze."

"That's your first mistake, Inspector," Novak replied, pacing the front of the room. "The Pink Panthers don't have a headquarters. They operate like a terrorist network—autonomous cells. There are roughly 200 to 800 core members, but they only activate for specific jobs. One cell might handle the 'Inside Man' recruitment, another the logistics, and a third—the 'Hit Team'—actually walks through the door. They share contacts, they share methods, but the man holding the gun often doesn't even know the name of the man who sold the stones."

"And the cross-dressing?" another officer asked, gesturing to the photo of the blonde wigs found in the getaway car. "It seems... unnecessary for military men."

"It's theater," Novak said flatly. "They use 'Shock and Awe.' They know the psychological profile of security guards. You see a woman in a blonde wig and high heels, you hesitate for two seconds. In a Pink Panther heist, two seconds is the difference between a locked door and a $100 million payday. They've hit Tokyo in three minutes and rammed Audis through malls in Dubai in under sixty seconds. They don't just rob you; they perform for you, and by the time you realize it's a play, they're across the border."

Visser pointed to a photo of a man with cold, predatory eyes. "What about Dragan Mikić? I've seen his name in the Interpol bulletins."

"Mikić is a legend in the Balkans," Novak nodded. "He scaled a prison wall while his associates provided cover fire with machine guns. He's the gold standard for their 'never-leave-a-man-behind' policy. But Mikić is a ghost. Right now, your ghost is **Douadi Yahiaoui**. He's the bridge between the Balkan muscle and the local French underworld. If he orchestrated the Harry Winston hit, he didn't do it for the thrill. He did it because he already had a buyer in Antwerp or Dubai before he even put on that wig."

The room went quiet as the weight of the task settled in. They weren't just chasing a group of robbers; they were chasing a military-grade ghost network that had successfully declared war on the world's most secure boutiques.

"They have no home, no fixed address, and they change identities as easily as they change wigs," Novak concluded, shutting off the projector. "The only thing they leave behind is a vacuum where the diamonds used to be. If you want to catch them, you have to stop thinking like a cop and start thinking like a soldier who has nothing left to lose."

Visser crushed his cigarette into a glass tray, the embers glowing one last time before dying out. "Then we stop looking for the diamonds," he said, his voice cold. "We start looking for the leak. Someone in that store invited the war inside. Find me the man who whispered the names."

Whisper of names

The realization didn't come with a "Eureka" moment in the middle of a raid; it began as a nagging itch in Chief Inspector Visser's mind during the very first witness debriefings. Every employee recounted the same terrifying detail: the thieves hadn't just barked orders; they had whispered names. *"Mickaël, the keys." "Don't move, Sophie."* To the victims, it was a terrifying display of omniscience. To Visser, it was a neon sign pointing toward a traitor. High-end thieves do their homework, but knowing the rotating shift schedule and the specific nicknames of floor staff required a level of intimacy that no long-range telescope could provide.

The BRB began a "Quiet Sweep" of the Harry Winston payroll. They weren't looking for a criminal mastermind; they were looking for a "Small Man"—someone with enough access to be dangerous but enough debt or resentment to be bought. They vetted the jewelers, the cleaners, and the management, but the focus inevitably shifted toward the security team. Among them was **Mouloud Djennad**, a man who had spent years guarding the very stones that had now vanished. On paper, he was unremarkable—a steady employee who knew the rhythms of the boutique like his own heartbeat.

"He's too clean," Visser's deputy muttered, tossing Djennad's file onto the desk. "No priors, no gambling debts, no sudden Ferraris in the driveway. If he's our guy, he's a professional at being invisible."

"Check his 'shadow' contacts," Visser replied, gesturing to a stack of cell phone tower logs. "I don't care about his bank account. I care about who he talks to when he thinks the lights are off. Nobody helps the Pink Panthers for free, and nobody does it without a handler."

The 9th Arrondissement is a place of two faces: by day, it is the grand home of the Opéra Garnier and bustling department stores; by night, it recedes into the shadows of the Pigalle, where the neon lights of "hostess bars" bleed into the damp pavement. It was here, in the back of a shuttered brasserie smelling of stale tobacco and floor wax, that Chief Inspector Visser waited. He wasn't there for the scenery. He was there for **"L'Araignée"—The Spider**—a mid-level fence who had spent decades weaving a web of illicit connections across the Parisian underworld.

The BRB had found the Spider through a "bottleneck" operation. Following the Harry Winston heist, Visser had ordered a total freeze on the movement of stolen luxury goods in the city. They squeezed every pawn shop, every back-alley jeweler, and every known broker until the black market began to suffocate. The Spider had been caught with a bag of "hot" Cartier watches from a separate robbery—a mistake that would normally cost him five years. But Visser didn't want the watches; he wanted the name of the man who had the audacity to hit the Avenue Montaigne.

"The coffee is cold, Patrick," the Spider murmured, sliding into the booth. His eyes, yellowed by years of cheap wine and late nights, scanned the empty street through the window. "And my lawyer is wondering why I'm sitting in a dark room with the head of the BRB instead of being processed at the station."

"Your lawyer is the least of your problems," Visser replied, his voice a low, steady threat. He slid a folder across the table. Inside were photos of the Spider's warehouse—a space filled with enough evidence to bury him for a decade. "The Harry Winston job has the Ministry of Justice breathing down my neck. That means I'm breathing down yours. If I don't get a lead tonight, you go into a cell and I lose the key."

The Spider looked at the folder, then back at Visser. The leverage was absolute. "The job was too big," the informant whispered, leaning in so close Visser could smell the garlic and anxiety on his breath. "The local boys are terrified. They say the men who did it aren't thieves—they're ghosts from the East. But ghosts need a place to haunt, don't they?"

"Give me a name," Visser demanded. "And you walk out of here with a clean slate on the watches. No charges, no record. A 'professional courtesy' from the Republic."

The Spider hesitated, his fingers drumming a nervous rhythm on the tabletop. "There's a man... a local heavy named **Douadi Yahiaoui**. He's been moving in circles he shouldn't be in. He's been seen with a man from the Balkans—a real 'Panther' type, tall, quiet, looks like he's seen a dozen wars. But that's not the part you'll find interesting."

"Go on," Visser urged, his hand hovering over his notebook.

"Yahiaoui has a friend," the Spider continued, his voice dropping to a barely audible rasp. "A 'little mouse' who works the doors at the Golden Triangle. He didn't give me a name, but he said the mouse was tired of watching billionaires buy stones the size of his fist while he lived on a guard's pittance. This mouse... he didn't just give them the codes. He gave them the heart of the store."

The Spider explained that the "inside man" had been recruited months prior in a gambling den in Saint-Denis. Yahiaoui had allegedly paid off the guard's debts in exchange for a "consultation" on the boutique's security vulnerabilities. The informant confirmed that the Pink Panthers didn't just stumble upon the names of the employees—they had been studying a "cheat sheet" provided by this traitor for weeks before the blonde wigs ever touched their heads.

"Where is Yahiaoui now?" Visser asked, his adrenaline finally spiking.

"He's playing it smart. Staying low in Pavillons-sous-Bois," the Spider replied, sliding a scrap of paper across the table with a handwritten address. "But he's got the 'Big Rocks' hidden. He's waiting for the heat to turn into ice before he moves them to Antwerp. You didn't hear it from me, Patrick. If the Panthers find out I talked, they won't send a lawyer—they'll send a grenade."

Visser stood up, pocketing the paper. He didn't thank the man; he simply nodded to the two plainclothes officers waiting by the door to let the Spider melt back into the night. The "rat" had given him the thread. All Visser had to do now was pull at the thread until the whole organization unraveled.

Sewer of Diamonds

The informant claimed Yahiaoui had been bragging about having a "mouse" inside the fortress. When the BRB ran a cross-reference between Yahiaoui's known associates and Djennad's phone records, the "invisible" man suddenly came into sharp focus.

A series of burner phone pings placed Djennad and a known associate of the Panthers in the same dingy bistro in the Parisian outskirts three weeks before the heist. While the rest of the world was looking for Serbian mercenaries, Djennad had been sipping espresso and handing over a hand-drawn map of the boutique's "blind spots" and the bypass codes for the secondary safes.

Visser authorized a "Pressure Play." They didn't arrest Djennad immediately; they put him under 24-hour surveillance, waiting for him to crack under the weight of the investigation. They watched him return to work at the now-empty boutique, his face a mask of professional concern as he held the door for the very detectives who were hunting him. It was a psychological game of chicken.

The crack finally appeared two months later. The surveillance team took up positions in a "clunker" van parked two blocks away from a modest house owned by Yahiaoui's family. For weeks, they watched. They saw men coming and going—tough, silent men with the scars of the Balkans on their faces and the weariness of the Parisian underworld in their eyes. They watched **Mouloud Djennad**, the Harry Winston security guard, meet Yahiaoui in a park. It was a brief handoff, a heavy envelope for a piece of paper. The "Inside Man" was finally on the hook. As Djennad walked away, his gait had changed; the military posture of a guard had slumped into the hurried shuffle of a man carrying a heavy secret.

Visser moved in that night. The arrest wasn't a grand spectacle; they picked him up as he was walking to his car after a shift. In the interrogation room, the "Inside Man" didn't hold out long. He wasn't a hardened Balkan soldier; he was a man who had been seduced by the promise of a life that his security salary could never provide.

"They told me nobody would get hurt," Djennad whispered, his head in his hands, the fluorescent lights reflecting off his pale skin. "They just wanted the stones. They said the insurance would pay for it all. I just... I just gave them the names."

"You didn't just give them names, Mouloud," Visser said, leaning into the man's space, his voice a low, dangerous rumble. "You gave them the floor plans, the schedules, and the lives of the people you worked with for years. You were the one who opened the door for the wolves. Now, tell me where Yahiaoui took the 'Big Rocks'."

After hours and days of interrogations it was beginning to be clear Djennad did not know where Yahiaoui stashed the valuables.

The BRB didn't have the diamonds, but they had something almost as valuable: a list of every burner phone that had pinged the towers near Avenue Montaigne on the day of the robbery. In a cramped, windowless room at the Quai des Orfèvres, a team of analysts lived on cold espresso and nicotine, listening to thousands of hours of intercepted "garbage" talk. Most of it was drug deals and domestic squabbles, but then, a voice they had been tracking—belonging to a known associate of **Douadi Yahiaoui**—said something that made the headphones go cold.

"The girl is sleeping in the rain," the voice whispered over a scrambled line. "She's deep, but she's dry."

Chief Inspector Visser, leaning over a technician's shoulder, felt the hair on his arms stand up. "Run that back," he commanded. To the uninitiated, it sounded like a code for a hidden body or a drug stash. But Visser knew the Pink Panther lore. They didn't bury bodies; they buried "girls"— their nickname for high-carat diamonds. The hunt moved from the glitz of the Golden Triangle to the gritty, grey suburbs of **Pavillons-sous-Bois**, northeast of Paris.

"We have enough for the snatch," Visser's deputy whispered into the radio as they watched Yahiaoui light a cigarette on his back porch. "No," Visser replied from the command center. "If we move now, the diamonds vanish. He's comfortable. He thinks the heat has died down. Let him lead us to the 'girl'."

The breakthrough came on a Tuesday morning in early 2011. Yahiaoui was seen in the backyard with a trowel and a bag of quick-dry cement. He wasn't gardening. He spent three hours working on a small patch of ground near the drainage pipe. To any neighbor, it looked like a routine repair to a leaking sewer line. To Visser, watching the high-resolution feed from a game camera hidden in a nearby tree, it was the "X" on the treasure map.

"Go," Visser finally barked into his headset. "Take the house. Take the yard. Nobody flushes anything."

The raid was a symphony of violence. Flashbangs shattered the suburban morning as GIPN commandos breached the front door. Yahiaoui was tackled before he could run inside. But as Visser stepped into the backyard, his heart sank. The yard was a mess of dirt and old pipes. It looked like a construction site, not a vault.

"Start digging," Visser ordered, gesturing toward the fresh cement. "And don't stop until you hit the sewer main."

For six hours, the detectives traded their pistols for shovels. The sun began to set, casting long, mocking shadows over the dirt. One officer, sweating through his tactical vest, struck something hard—not the hollow sound of metal pipe, but the dull thud of a heavy container.

"Chief! I've got something!"

Visser dropped into the hole, his fingers clawing at the mud. He pulled out a large, airtight plastic container, sealed with industrial-grade tape and encased in a block of set concrete. He used a tactical knife to pry it open. Inside, wrapped in common kitchen foil, was a sight that made the entire team go silent.

A pair of earrings—white gold, encrusted with diamonds the size of thumbnails—glimmered even in the failing light. Beside them, a necklace worth more than the entire street of houses. It was $20 million of the Harry Winston haul, literally pulled from the filth of a suburban drain.

Visser held up a massive ring, the center stone catching the light. "Found her," he whispered. "She was just taking a bath."

But as he looked at the haul, his brow furrowed. The "Sewer of Diamonds" was a massive win, but it was only a fraction of the $100 million stolen. The "Big Rocks"—the legendary stones that Novak had warned them about—were missing. The trail didn't end in the sewer; it was leading straight back to the Balkan mountains.

Heist of the Century

The trial began in February 2015, nearly seven years after the blonde wigs had first crossed the threshold of Number 29 Avenue Montaigne. The courtroom in Paris was a theater of high-stakes tension, filled with the heavy presence of armed gendarmes and the sharp scent of old paper. In the glass-walled dock sat eight men—the remnants of a conspiracy that had successfully executed the "Heist of the Century."

Chief Inspector Visser watched from the gallery as **Douadi Yahiaoui**, the alleged mastermind, sat with a look of defiant boredom. Beside him, **Mouloud Djennad**, the former security guard, looked like a ghost of the man he once was. The prosecution didn't just have the jewelry found in the sewer; they had the "Balkan Thread"—a trail of satellite phone pings and encrypted messages that led from the suburbs of Paris straight into the jagged peaks of the **Balkan Mountains**.

"The reach of this organization does not end at the borders of France," the lead prosecutor, Marie-Claire Dubois, declared, pacing before the judges. "Through the cooperation of Interpol and Serbian authorities, we tracked the 'Big Rocks'—the legendary diamonds that vanished from the safe. They didn't go to Antwerp. They were moved through a 'ratline' into Montenegro, protected by men who treat war like a hobby and theft like a profession."

The trial reached its peak when Djennad was called to testify. The room fell into a suffocating silence. "Why?" Dubois asked, her voice echoing in the chamber. "You had a life. A career. Why betray the people who stood beside you every day?" Djennad looked at his hands, his voice a broken whisper. "I saw more wealth in one afternoon at that store than my family would see in ten lifetimes. Yahiaoui... he made it sound like justice. He said the insurance would pay, and I would finally be able to breathe. I didn't realize that once you open the door for the Panthers, you can never close it again."

Yahiaoui's lawyer fought back with the ferocity of a cornered animal, pointing to the lack of physical evidence linking the Balkan leadership directly to the Paris cell. "You have a few stones from a sewer and the word of a terrified guard," he sneered. "Where are the hundreds of millions in diamonds? Where are the so-called 'Commanders' of the Panthers? You are putting ghosts on trial because you cannot find the men."

The tension broke when a surprise witness—a Serbian investigator from the "Project Pink Panther" task force—took the stand. He produced a series of photographs taken via long-range surveillance in a remote village near the Bosnian border. They showed a man identified as a high-ranking Panther associate holding a distinct, unmounted pear-shaped diamond. The diamond matched the specifications of one of Harry Winston's most prized missing pieces.

"The diamonds are no longer stones," the Serbian investigator explained coldly. "They have been recut in clandestine workshops. They are now 'new' gems, circulating in the markets of Dubai and Hong Kong. The $80 million that is missing isn't lost; it has simply changed its face."

The verdict was a hammer blow. **Douadi Yahiaoui** was sentenced to **15 years**. **Mouloud Djennad** received **2 years**—a light sentence only because his confession had cracked the case wide open. Other accomplices were handed sentences ranging from 9 months to 12 years. As the defendants were led away, Yahiaoui caught Visser's eye and offered a thin, mocking smile. He knew, as the police knew, that the core of the Pink Panthers remained untouched, likely planning their next "performance" from a villa in the mountains.

The Harry Winston heist remains a masterclass in criminal audacity. While the BRB recovered a fraction of the loot from the filth of a suburban sewer, the "Big Rocks" remain ghosts—shining reminders of a twenty-minute window where the most expensive street in Paris belonged to the Panthers.

Sources:

BBC News. "Jewels Found in Paris Sewer." Last modified March 8, 2011. https://www.bbc.com/news/world-europe-12674482.

Chrisafis, Angelique. "Trial of Eight Men Accused of 'Heist of the Century' at Paris Jewellers." *The Guardian*, February 2, 2015. https://www.theguardian.com/world/2015/feb/02/harry-winston-jewellery-heist-paris-trial-eight-men.

Erlanger, Steven. "Eight Sentenced in 2008 Paris Jewelry Heist." *The New York Times*, February 27, 2015. https://www.nytimes.com/2015/02/28/world/europe/eight-sentenced-in-2008-paris-jewelry-heist.html.

Interpol. "Pink Panthers." Accessed May 22, 2024. https://www.interpol.int/en/Crimes/Organized-crime/Pink-Panthers.

Le Monde with AFP. "Huit hommes jugés pour le 'casse du siècle' chez Harry Winston." *Le Monde*, February 2, 2015. https://www.lemonde.fr/police-justice/article/2015/02/02/huit-hommes-juges-pour-le-casse-du-siecle-chez-harry-winston_4567926_1653578.html.

Samuels, David. "The Pink Panthers: A Story of Diamonds, Thieves, and the Balkans." *The New Yorker*, July 12, 2010. https://www.newyorker.com/magazine/2010/07/19/the-pink-panthers.

Note on Dramatization

While the narrative provided in our session adheres to the factual timeline of the December 2008 robbery, the 2011 recovery, and the 2015 trial, specific elements were dramatized for storytelling:

- **Dialogue:** Known quotes (such as the use of staff names and the "Pink Panther" cold cream origin) are documented facts. Transitionary dialogue and the internal thoughts of investigators (e.g., "Chief Inspector Visser") were fabricated to maintain the suspenseful tone requested.
- **Character Archetypes:** While the "Spider" and specific interrogations are representative of the methods used by the **Brigade de Répression du Banditisme (BRB)**, the specific meeting in the 9th Arrondissement was a narrative construction of documented investigative techniques.

About the Author

Ric Oro

Ric is a writer who prefers to let the facts speak for themselves. With a keen eye for detail and a lifelong fascination with the world's most daring heists, he specializes in bringing complex true crime and financial mysteries to life for a younger audience. He spends much of his time researching the stories that others have forgotten, always searching for the next great truth hidden behind a locked vault.

For more information visit the Youtube channel for shorts on true crime stories and sneak peeks of future volumes:

https://www.youtube.com/@ShadowRamMedia

www.ingramcontent.com/pod-product-compliance
Lightning Source LLC
Chambersburg PA
CBHW020006290326
41935CB00007B/325